Marie Robinson Wright

Salvador

Marie Robinson Wright

Salvador

ISBN/EAN: 9783337118266

Printed in Europe, USA, Canada, Australia, Japan

Cover: Foto ©Andreas Hilbeck / pixelio.de

More available books at **www.hansebooks.com**

SALVADOR

General Carlos Ezeta

Señora Ezeta

SALVADOR

(ILLUSTRATED)

BY

Marie Robinson Wright

PUBLISHED BY

L'ARTISTE PUBLISHING CO.,

NEW YORK.

PRINT OF
L'ARTISTE PUBLISHING CO.
7 WARREN ST., N. Y.

DEDICATION

I am greatly honored in the privilege of dedicating this record of my visit to Salvador to President Carlos Ezeta and General Antonio Ezeta—*Par Nobile Fratrum*. Illustrious alike, yet diverse, both superbly endowed.

"Now there are diversities of gifts but the same spirit," and between these two there exists a beautiful harmony—the highest type of fraternity. Their splendid prowess in war is matched by their conceptions and achievements in peace, and their courage and wisdom have made their Republic the cynosure of civilized nations.

(1) DR. DON DAVID CASTRO.
(5) DR. DON ESTEVAN CASTRO.
(3) DR. DON DOMINGO JAIMENEZ.
(6) DR. DON NICOLAS ANGULO.
(4) GENERAL CARLOS EZETA, President of Salvador.
(2) GENERAL ANTONIO EZETA, Vice-President of Salvador.

SALVADOR

Like a glorious tropic flower thrown upon the pulsing tide of the peaceful ocean, Salvador rests upon the Pacific. It is located in Central America, bordered by Honduras, Guatemala and Nicaragua, and its sea front measures one hundred and thirty-nine miles. It is bounded on the north by Honduras and Guatemala; on the east by Honduras and the Gulf of Fonesca, which separates it from Nicaragua; on the south by the Pacific Ocean, and on the west by Guatemala. It is a land of great present prosperity and illimitable resources and possibilities.

The approaches to this jewel of a Republic are wonderfully novel and enchanting. The gradual floating down into the tropics is a sensation restful and full of an unreal and dream-like charm. It is almost too marvelous, too beautiful to be true! Our first sight of these magical shores was like that of a noted traveler: "The sky was ruddy, the air fresh and invigorating, but soft as the gates of Paradise. We were in the tropics. You would have known it with your eyes shut; the whole wonderful atmosphere con-

fessed it. But with your eyes open, those white birds sailing like snow-flakes
through the immaculate blue heavens, with tail-feathers like our pennant, the
floating gardens of the sea through which we had been ruthlessly ploughing
for a couple of days back; the gorgeous sunrises and sunsets—all were positive
proofs positive of our latitude."

This gives one a sense of spiritual enlargement and freedom, but the
body is soon to be imprisoned in the most wonderful of all landing appliances. The ships anchor several miles off the coast, at the port of La
Libertad, or Acajutla, and passengers and freight are transported to the long
out-jutting piers by launches. Here you are by no means landed, as you have
yet to be caged and swung to the platform. As you sit in your lighter you
see descending from above a huge iron cage or elevator. This holds six
people. It plumps down into your boat and you are asked to step in. As
soon as it receives its proper number the boatman shuts the door and signals
the engineer on the landing above—oh, so far above!—and you are swung
out over the tossing waves like a scrap of paper in a gale. Almost before
you have time to realize the distance, you are raised with a swing and a
swoop; it lands you on the blessed, solid platform. The sensation is extremely novel, but the transit is brief and no accidents ever happen to the
flying cage.

The history of Salvador is an inspiring one, filled with the records of
the deeds of dauntless men and tragic eras, all tending to the gradual civilization and enlightenment in affairs of both church and State that make the
little republic of to-day so alluring to the traveler, so full of promise to the
settler and investor. For not only is it a land of delightful tradition and
physical beauty, but it abounds in splendid resources, many of which are still
in a virgin or undeveloped state. The earliest inhabitants known to the his-
torian were the Aztecas and Nahautls, the same races that founded Nicaragua
and the other republics of Central America and the Mexican Empire. Over
three centuries of association with the whites, and the influence of long
Spanish domination, has, of course, vastly changed, if not obliterated, the
characteristics of the aboriginal population, yet there are certain sections where
the primitive traits, customs and tongue have been retained to a surprising

VOLCANO OF IZALCO SALVADOR.

degree. This shows itself especially in the names of places, which in some instances are almost the same in spelling and pronunciation that they were nearly four centuries ago. The clinging to old speech and old ways is more marked in that portion of the republic known as *Costa del Balsimo*, or Balsam Coast. Here many of the old rites and usages prevail. It is the stronghold of the balsam product, which is very valuable, but extremely rare. This territory is a strip of land lying along the coast, between the ports of Acajulta and La Libertad. It is situated to the seaward from the volcanic range, and consists of an extensive forest of balsam trees. These aboriginals have a monopoly of this industry, are supported entirely by it; and live in unmolested seclusion. They are extremely clannish, and while they visit the outer world for purposes of barter and trade when necessary, they do not invite or even countenance visitors to their forest fastnesses. They live on the co-operative or community plan—all their earnings are given in charge of old men, called *ahaules*, who are not only treasurers, but priests, and keep sacred both the altar and the strong-box of the nation. These wise counsellors are all powerful in their administration of the public moneys, and they decide the needs of each family and distribute the funds accordingly. There is a belief throughout the republic that this tribe is possessed of a vast treasure of money, as their revenues are large and their needs exceedingly simple; and the tradition exists to the effect that their surplus income is buried once a year with sacred and secret ceremonials. Those who have caught glimpses of them in their forest seclusion report that both sexes go entirely nude, save for a breech clout, but when they appear in the towns they are clothed in the cotton costumes usual to the peones. They are dark in color, large in stature, silent, unsocial, dignified, said to be temperate in their habits, hard working, honorable in their dealings with others and peaceful among themselves. They are called Balsimos. They plant just enough grains and other vegetable crops for their own use. They number only about twenty-two hundred, and are supposed to sell between twenty and thirty thousand dollars worth of balsam each year. Their festivals and religious ceremonies are said to be extremely barbaric. The balsam trees are treated after the manner of our pines in the turpentine industry, though, of course, without the aid of modern appliances.

The hardened product is wrapped in leaves and sent to market. It goes by the name of Peruvian balsam, as the first known to commerce came from Peru, but the supply now is derived exclusively from the Balsimos of Salvador.

This balsam is very rarely found by strangers seeking the wonderful tree. The natives alone know of its existence, its peculiarities and its properties. I know from personal observation that it cannot be found even by medical experts who claim to know it at sight. The secret is born with the natives, and they guard it with their lives. Yet in New York and in other large cities it is found, shipped by these Indians yearly.

Way back as far as history reaches, and where it is hardly to be distinguished from tradition, the land now known as Salvador was said to have been well peopled and to have had large towns and villages built of lime and stone. The original name of the country was Cuscatlan, which meant "Tierra de prefeas o' freseas,"—land of riches—which refers to its beauty, the fertility and variety of its soil products, as well as to its precious minerals, as *Cuscatl* is the original for jewels or valuable gems, In ancient times the people were ruled by local chiefs, and the country at large seemed to have no king or chief ruler. They had a kind of organized priesthood and many religious feasts and ceremonials. They worshipped the sun and had idols to whom they made sacrifice. Their rites were similar to those of others of the Aztecs in their barbarity and the frequent sacrifice of human victims. Immorality was punished by whipping, robbers were banished from the country, and murderers were killed by being thrown from a high rock.

Although Alvarado reported the finding of substantial cities and towns, there is little left now to confirm his statements, and these consist mainly of mounds, terraces, towers and subterranean galleries, with here and there long stretches of city walls, with occasional carvings and sculptures.

San Salvador, the noble capital of the republic, is eighteen miles from the coast, and has an elevation of 2800 feet. Its neighbors are volcanoes, two of them being active. Yzalco is the king of the group, and is constantly sending forth his flaming and thunderous proclamations. When in full eruption this burning peak is a sight of inexpressible awe and grandeur.

It is called "*El Faro del Salvador*" "The Lighthouse of Salvador." San Salvador was founded by Alvarado, a brother of the great Cortez. It occupies a most commanding and beautiful situation. It is located on a grand

Church Ruin OF IZALCO SALVADOR OVER 150 YEARS OLD

mountain plain, or table land, facing the sea on the south, and girdled by lofty ranges on the three other sides. The climate is delicious, as the prevailing winds come laden with the vigor and coolness of the sea. Besides, the streams in its neighborhood are many, and nature is always verdant and fresh. The water system through the streets is complete, and in this way gardens are kept green and luxurious, and the tinkle of fountains plays a soft accompaniment to the murmur of city sounds. The dwellings, for the most part, are of one story, not imposing from the outside, but marvels of tropic

CHURCH IN SANTA ANA SALVADOR

OVER 400 YEARS OLD.   CHURCH IN CHALCHUAPA SALVADOR

comfort inside, and all supplied with the open court, or patio, where trees, hammocks and falling waters make life a dream of oriental restfulness.

The cathedral is magnificent in proportions and decorations, colored tiles, gilding and paintings. The President's palace is an abode befitting his dignity and rank, and there are many other buildings imposing and attractive that are shown in my illustrations. In church the women do not wear hats or bonnets, but the more graceful high combs, gold pins and lace mantillas. They light up the cathedral, these flashing visions of black hair, cream-like complexions and love-lit eyes. They love color, jewelry and lace, and wear costly chains of gold and ropes of pearls. The poorer classes are scarcely less picturesque—the men barefoot, in baggy trousers and braided jackets, and the women garbed in gay skirts with snow-white blouses or chemises low-necked and short-sleeved. One feels in looking at this radiant people so full of light and color that they could never be reproduced by pencil, pastel or the neutral shades employed by the photographer. Only the richest oils could give an idea of their superb coloring, or, better still, the tints filched from the rainbow or from the flying glory of autumn leaves.

The Constitution gives the legislative power to the National Assembly, composed of three deputies from each of the fourteen departments, or forty-two in all, allowing two alternates for each department. This assembly is renewed every year, the election taking place on the first Sunday in January, and all members are eligible to re-election. The judicial power rests in a supreme court, composed of eleven magistrates, and other primary and secondary courts and justices of the peace.

The administration of the affairs of state are vested in a President, who is elected, by general suffrage, for four years. He appoints four ministers to conduct the different branches of the government. At this time the chief ruler of the republic is President Carlos Ezeta, and his Cabinet are: Dr. Don David Castro, Dr. Don Esteran Castro, Dr. Don Domingo Jaimenez, Dr. Don Nicolas Angulo and General Antonio Ezeta.

San Salvador has, of course, a public park. It is handsomely laid out, and is embowered with splendid palms, bread-fruit trees, bananas, cacti and other large-leafed and flowering trees. The paths are paved and bordered

INTERIOR VIEWS HOTEL - SAN SALVADOR.

with blooming things, and the outer rim of the entire *pleasaunce* is enriched with a double row of orange trees, always a royal sight, in leaf, blossom and fruitage.   Here a well-conducted band plays a choice program of classic music two nights in the week, and these occasions are general festivals to the music-loving populace.   The park has an ample supply of seats, summer houses and pagodas and is well lighted.   Here the music of the Spanish tongue rivals the melody of the orchestra, the eyes of the native beauties put to shame the artificial lights, and the filmy smoke of the cigarette, puffed from rosy feminine lips, mingles with the odors of the flowers.

Along the country roads there is much to charm the eye of the traveler. Palms, "those exclamation points in the poetry of tropic landscapes;" glossy coffee-bushes, bananas with their red and yellow fruit, oranges, spheres of gold and stars of sweetest perfume; sugar cane (a stately plant), maize and other flourishing grains.   Here and there are palm-thatched huts, now and then a more luxurious mansion, strange old-fashioned carts and carriages, the latter drawn by three mules harnessed abreast; processions on muleback—all these are seen, with enchanting vistas, glimpsed through long well-kept hedges and glorious bits of scenery—now a rich valley; now a volcanic peak; now a range of amethystine mountains—everywhere beauty, abundance, grandeur!   "This," says a delighted traveler, "was Arcadia shut in by jealous Nature from the rest of the world.   This was Utopia surviving in rustic quiet and sylvan simplicity, life and long feast derived from the riches yielded by an exuberant and grateful soil."

The traveler in Salvador will be impressed by the unfailing and exquisite courtesy of the people. They are ever willing to give aid, information, or to bestow charming gifts in the way of flowers, *dulces* and other products of the country.   The ruling impulse seems to be one of generous hospitality, and their phrases convey so much kindliness, so much good will, that their greetings have a flavor of genuine homage.   The working people are just as polite as the aristocracy, and no laboring man passes a lady on the streets without raising his hat.   In the country highways and byways the salutations are even more cordial and personal, and one is often greeted with words of blessing and cheer, thus: "May your patron saint protect you from danger;"

"May Heaven smile upon your path;" "May the Blessed Virgin watch over your journey;" all this couched in the soft, melodious syllables of the sweet tongue derived from the Spanish:

> "The talk of Spanish men
> With Southern intonation, vowels turned
> Caressingly between the consonants,
> Persuasive, willing, with such intervals
> As music borrows from the wooing birds
> That plead with subtly curving swift descent."

The feasts of the Salvadorians are peculiarly interesting. They celebrate many days of patriotic importance, anniversaries of historical events. There is no half-way or half-hearted joining in these occasions. The enthusiasm is warm and general. All places of business are closed, and the entire population given over to merry-making. The streets are brilliantly and profusely decorated, high mass is celebrated in the morning, and the day is devoted to patriotic speeches, processions, music and universal glorification, and at night there are suppers, fireworks, balls and banquets 'til the stars fade into the roseate dawn. The grand feast days of all the year are Christmas and the day of the patron saint, Saint Michael—or San Miguel. These are largely religious, with the inevitable mixture of fairs, fire-works and out-of-door pastimes. At Christmas the gayeties partake somewhat of the nature of a carnival, and bon-bons, floral offerings and egg-shells filled with perfume, are tossed about in the crowd. Christmas trees are a feature, and in many houses a room is fitted up to portray the manger and *Naciamento,* or birth of the Saviour. These representations are very realistic and impressive. A great display is made at the Cathedral, where there are long and magnificient ceremonies, a vast outlay of money in lights and decorations and a wonderful service of music, at which not only the leading orchestras and vocalists of the country assist, but the military bands also. The most beautiful woman in the city is posed as the Virgin, and this selection is esteemed an exalted honor.

The markets in a strange country are always points of attraction, as it is here that one sees the people face to face, in their native dress, and receives valuable impressions of their customs and of the products of the

RUIN IN SAN SALVADOR, SALVADOR.

SUGAR PLANTATION, GUATEMALA

country. In San Salvador it is near the Cathedral. It is a rambling building, floored with cement. Here strange fruits, flowers, vegetables, birds, handwork are to be bought at temptingly low prices. Outside of the building, the Indian vendors are ranged, their goods displayed in an enticing manner, which is enhanced by their agreeable and smiling solicitations. All is good-humored rivalry and gentleness, and though these dark-eyed, dark-skinned hucksters are presumably badly off in this world's goods, their air is so serene that one thinks "their ways (*must*) be ways of pleasantness, and their paths be paths of peace."

It is an established fact that there are many circumstances which powerfully contribute both towards the development of a country's material resources and its advancement on the high roads of civilization, but at the same time, it cannot be denied that there are necessary men whose character and abilities determine a marked progress on a nation's destiny, and where brilliant career and worthy deeds impress their seal on the historical period that witnessed their success.

The two foremost figures in the history of Salvador are Carlos and Antonio Ezeta, the president and vice-president of this Republic. These two brothers have by their patriotism, courage and many attributes, won the affection and admiration of their countrymen, who regard them as "the Siamese brothers of valor, patriotism and glory." Carlos Ezeta was born in San Salvador, on the 14th of June, 1853; his parents being Colonel Eligio Ezeta, and Dona Asuncion de Leon. After mastering the rudiments of an education, he was placed under the tutelage of the Spanish General, Luis Perez Gomez, director of the National Military Academy, who took charge of his technical training. While here, a mere cadet, Carlos saved the life of the then President of Salvador, Don Francisco Duenas, which was threatened by the revolutionists under General Santiago Gonzales. In 1872, young Ezeta was transferred to the Guard of Honor of Marshal Gonzales, as a lieutenant. While holding this commission, his young soul, hungry for glory, he offered his services to Honduras, and fought against the government of General Medina until it was overthrown. His bravery made him a first lieutenant, and in 1873 he earned his captain's bars, after having won distinction and

WATER FALL NEAR SALVADO

renown. After the death of General Espinosa, in June, 1875, under whom he had served, he went to Nicaragua and Costa Rica, where he stayed in voluntary exile for a year. On his return to Salvador, in 1876, at the outset of the administration of Zaldivar, he was appointed military instructor of the garrison of San Salvador, ranking as lieutenant-colonel. This was the only era in Zaldivar's term, when the republic had really any regular troops—this being due to Ezeta's ability and discipline.

As the result of a conspiracy against Zaldivar, in which Carlos Ezeta was engaged, he was expatriated with many of his comrades in arms. This exile was a modern odyssey, ranging through strange lands and beset by adventures and hardships. From New Orleans he went to Belize, where he took passage in an open boat for Guatemala. His negro boatmen robbed him of everything and abandoned him on the island of Stancreke. From here he sailed in a small craft for Livingston, Guatemala, being tossed into that port at midnight in a howling storm. He made his way into the interior where he remained several years, and won confidence and esteem by his courage and industry. In 1885, he joined General Rufino Barrios, in the Unionist campaign, that came to its tragic end at Chalchuapa. In this campaign, as brigadier-general, at the head of the Guatemalan forces, he fought the Salvadorians under General Monterrosa, and drove him from San Lorenzo and Las Pozas. At this time, the revolution led by General Francisco Menendez developed, and General Carlos Ezeta was the soul and right arm of the movement. He wrote his fame on many bloody fields, and when, on June 22, 1885, General Menendez entered the capital victorious, his first act was to make his brilliant assistant (Ezeta) Commandant and Military Governor of San Vicente. In 1886 General Ezeta, who, while in Guatemala, had met his first defeat and surrendered to a lovely daughter of that country, returned to Guatemala and married her. When he reached home he was made General in command of the Department of Santa Ana and Inspector-General of the Army. While in this office he made a brilliant record, and in 1889 stamped out the revolution of Cojutepec. His splendid courage and his constant successes in warfare enthralled his countrymen, and the Presidency was the reward tendered to him. On June 22, 1890, General Menendez, then President, had determined to exile Ezeta to prevent his becoming his successor. This plot reached the ears of his (Ezeta's) comrades-in-arms, and they at once decided to proclaim him their leader and install him in the Presidential chair. At nine o'clock on the night of June 22d, the brave General went to the artillery barracks in San Salvador and captured it single-handed, the troops there joining his cause. After a hard struggle his followers triumphed, and on the 23d of June he was proclaimed the head of the provisional government. Soon afterward, General Firnés, who was in command of three thousand men at San Miguel, tried to make them revolt, but as soon as it was known that he intended to march on the capital his brigade, to the last man, refused to go, and attacked and severely wounded him.

When Ezeta assumed executive control stagnation reigned in the republic, commerce was lifeless, industry dormant. The treasury was increasing its liabilities, agriculture languished, the army was disorganized, want was universal. Surrounding himself with wise assistants he said: "I do not wish to make a government of idlers; my government is and shall be essentially one of reconstruction, of work and of progress." To-day Salvador illustrates his wisdom and zeal. In all branches of trade and labor his clear and strong mind are to be traced. He has put the seal of his invincible character on all things. He is a frank, cordial and polished gentleman. His physique is attractive and his moral attributes noble. As a testimony to his unselfishness and bravery we copy a telegram sent to his brother at the front during the revolution of 1890:

"*General Antonio Ezeta:* I presume that by this time my dear wife and tender children are in the hands of my cowardly enemies, but even if you should find them slaughtered in the trenches do not hold back, but pass over them, if need be, to save the country. Your brother, CARLOS."

There spoke the patriot, a lover, husband, an adoring father; but before all, and above all, a hero!

The life of Antonio Ezeta is a romance dramatized, an epic poem set to martial music. His deeds, particularly those of his military career, are heroic and glorious. His brother Carlos was a soldier by education. Antonio was born a son of Mars. Grandly endowed as to mental powers, he has by energy and close application made a name in the field of letters, and writes with vigor wedded to grace. In the dark days of exile and deprivation he dedicated himself to hard, manual labor with the same calm determination that marks his efforts to-day in the elevated work to which he consecrates his talents. In him who, in these severe privations of exile, kept time to the oars, with songs that were memories of home, there will be found the

CHURCH IN SANTA TECLA SALVADOR.

same intrepid, high-souled man who now fills lofty stations and is a moulder of the destinies of his people. Antonio Ezeta was born on the 13th of June, 1855, and since his early boyhood he has shown many of the characteristics which have made him the great and glorious statesman of to-day.

In the campaign of 1873, in which his brother Carlos served as adjutant on the staff of General Espirnoza, Antonio was sub-lieutenant. As young as he was then; he was a warrior, and at Villa de la Paz he fought grandly in the hottest of the fray. The same year, at the terrible seven days' siege of Comayagua, he won his first lieutenancy by his distinguished gallantry. In 1876, in the campaign against Guatemala, his bravery made him captain. In this campaign he was severely wounded. Not favoring the policy of Zaldivar's administration, he went to Nicaragua, where for a year he taught school and acted as town clerk. He then went to Honduras, where General Delgado made him his adjutant. Later, President Soto, seeing and appreciating his rare worth and military talents, appointed him a lieutenant-colonel. A misunderstanding caused him to go to Gracias, Honduras, and accept a government position. Here, in 1879, he was involved in a revolt against the Soto administration, and after many daring achievements he was captured, shamefully flogged and kept in solitary confinement. After some months he escaped in a tobacco canoe and made his way, penniless, to Chinandega, Nicaragua. Scorning no honest service, this eminent man takes a noble pride in relating the adventures of this portion of his career. He varied his labor with literary pursuits and wrote many noteworthy articles for the papers. The most celebrated one, entitled "Nationality," caused his expulsion from Nicaragua in 1885. From thence he went to Costa Rica, sleeping nightly, en route, in the jails, where he was harshly treated on account of the above-named article. Shortly after reaching Puntarenas, in Costa Rica, he was arrested as an agent of Barrios, who had just issued his decree proclaiming the Central American Union. Ezeta was forced to march thirty leagues on weary feet to San José, where he was held in close confinement until the death of Barrios. On his release and return to Salvador he joined forces with Menendez in the revolution which vanquished Zaldivar and ended in May, 1885. He was now a colonel and at the head of the first regiment of the army stationed at San Salvador. For three years he was Commandant of the port of Acajutla, or until the revolution of June, 1890, conceived and consummated by his fearless brother Carlos.

During this revolution Antonio Ezeta, now a General, exhibited his superb military genius and made every movement a brilliant success. It is told of him that one night one of his colonels aroused him from a sound

Patio del hotel Nuevo Mundo

STREET SCENE. 9ᵀᴴ STR. ROW.
SAN SALVADOR. SALVADOR.

slumber and said: "General, we are lost, we are in a hole, in a blind alley, without means of egress. See! the heights are bristling with men." Antonio Ezeta replied, calmly: "If you are assailed with fear, return by the road; go home. You are relieved from all engagements. As for myself, I am resolved, and twenty-five men will serve to open a way. They may defeat me, but not without Central America first trembling." He is a man of great determination and perfect faith in himself, which the following proves:

On the 29th of July, 1890, General Ezeta found himself on the Guatemalan frontier fighting with 5000 Salvadoreans against 30,000 Guatemalans, when he received a telegram from his brother as to the treachery of General Rivas. To this he made reply: "Within forty hours I shall have recovered the capital and punished the traitor." And he kept his word!

When General Carlos Ezeta was elected President of Salvador, his brother Antonio was appointed Minister of War and the Interior. Owing to the state of his health, he was forced to resign in a short time, and went to Santa Ana to live, retaining only his commission as Major General in the army. It was not long, however, before the grateful memory of his distinguished services made him, by popular vote, the Vice-President. Like Cincinnatus returned to his plow when no longer lured by the clarion note of war, Antonio Ezeta has hung his sword upon the wall and dedicated his powers to the arts of peace. Antonio Ezeta now wields the pen, and at his magic touch there streams forth light, progress, harmony and union. His favorite themes, upon which he writes most eloquently, are the Central American union and permanent peace.

Since the new administration of Carlos and Antonio Ezeta, many laws have been introduced that tend to aid in the development of agriculture and mining industries. All modern improvements that tend to make a country powerful have been brought here for the first time, and order prevails everywhere. There are fine military schools established in San Miguel, Santa Ana and Salvador. The army, the pride of the whole country, is composed of fifty thousand well-drilled and disciplined soldiers, comfortably garrisoned and magnificently uniformed. I had the pleasure of seeing this grand army in one of their monthly reviews, in well-formed lines, at their noted park, Campo del

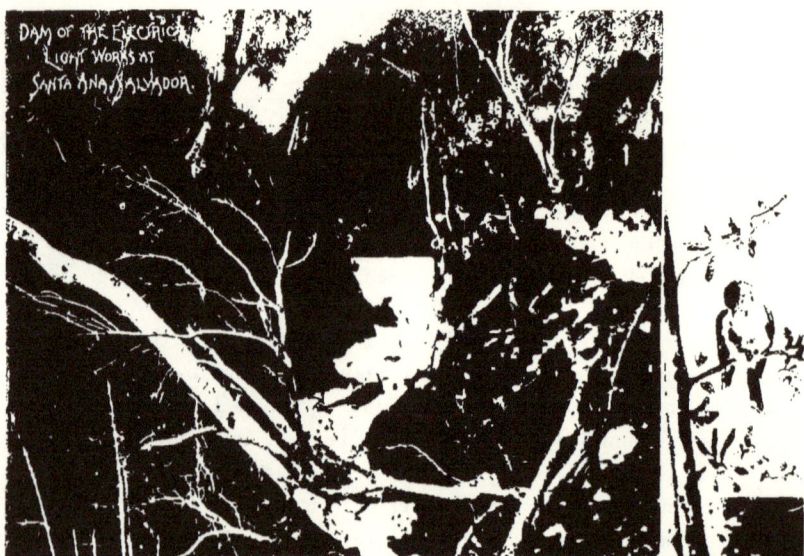

DAM OF THE ELECTRIC
LIGHT WORKS AT
SANTA ANA, SALVADOR.

WATER FLUME OF ELECTRIC LIGHT WORKS
AT SANTA ANA, SALVADOR.

Mars. It was a magnificent sight seldom beheld. Keeping the magic step and commanded by Central America's greatest General, Salvador's army echoes volumes of credit to its noble President and Chief.

It was through these powerful rulers that new roads were built, new parks made, telegraphs from State to State, telephone from city to city; in fact this whole administration has been one of progress. They have proven themselves worthy of the love and respect of their compatriots. They have guaranteed all the constitutional rights of their fellow-citizens. They have made a practical fact of the independence of the judicial and legislative bodies, and have introduced into Congress many laws to protect and help in all development. Without once recurring to the dictatorial measures born of ambitious views, they have managed to keep a peaceful country, and, now free from the ravages of war, Salvador flourishes, a glorious example of good discipline and government.

And so it is, their countrymen will ever cherish the memory of exploits and valor, energy and pluck when the days of war seemed darkest, striving and struggling for freedom of a country beloved and fought for with the spirit of the Spartans, whose motto was to return with the shield or on it. Their names will be recorded in Salvador's history, and posterity will know of the fathers of their prosperity. They are not only first to plunge into heated battle when the country is threatened with war, but they have been called the advocates of peace in time of peace, and thus endeared to the hearts of their countrymen, they now reign as magistrates over a land that commands the peace and respect of all the world.

Another of the most eminent diplomats of Salvador is Eduardo Poirier, who at the present writing is representing his republic at the Court of Mexico. He is a gentleman of ability and force, extremely affable and courtly in manner and of most attractive and graceful appearance. He has added greatly to the pleasure of the stranger within the gates of Mexico during his residence in that brilliant capital. Through his influence several important treaties have been concluded between Mexico and Salvador.

FOREIGN DEBT—The total foreign debt of Salvador, in May, 1893, was $3,614,000, or $5.16 1-3 per capita of population—a splendid showing, truly.

If the wealth of a country consists in the saving made after satisfying its necessities, Salvador is well justified in considering herself prosperous, since she produces much more than she consumes, as may be seen from the following statement giving the imports and exports for the five years from 1885 to 1889 inclusive:

	1885.	1886.	1887.	1888.	1889.
Imports	$2,134,095	$2,427,643	$3,343,520	$4,076,404	$2,878,000
Exports	5,716,428	4,754,649	5,242,607	6,707,024	5,489,000

Total exports in five years.................................... $27,909,798
Total imports in five years........... 14,859,962

This shows that after satisfying her necessities Salvador has saved $13,049,836, or an amount four times greater than her total foreign debt.

In December, 1892, Salvador bonds, which theretofore brought only fifty per cent., were being sought in London at seventy-five per cent. But Salvador might pay off her entire foreign debt, did she so desire, by the sale of the national railway, seventy miles in length, which has always been a lucrative business speculation, paying a good interest on the capital invested.

PUBLIC INSTRUCTION—Education is compulsory in the Republic, and the best efforts of the Government are being put forward to establish primary and other schools throughout its territory. During the year 1892 there were open 585 public schools for both sexes, with an attendance of 29,427 students. The number of teachers employed was 793. This does not represent all the public schools, as a number were closed in various parts of the Republic. The expense to the Government for the support of public schools, libraries, etc., during the year 1892 was $308,382.50. There are, besides the foregoing, ten private primary and grammar schools in Salvador, with a fair attendance, which are founded under the provisions of the laws regarding public instruction, and which are subsidized by the Government.

MINES—Salvador has numerous deposits of gold, silver, copper, iron, lead, plumbago, zinc, coal, marbles, quicksilver, opals, asbestos, etc. In the eastern section of the country there are several important mines, among which may be mentioned the Loma Larga, Corosal, Encuentros and Tabanco, which have yielded considerable quantities of gold and silver, leaving no doubt that with better systems of exploitation prevailing their product would be largely increased.

The great iron district is Metapan, to the west of the country. Unfortunately, the working of this metal is done by the old Catalan method, for which reason the success which should attach to mining in that territory is not achieved. To the north of Salvador, in the Department of Cabañas, there have been discovered several veins of precious metals and copper.

Coal mines have been also discovered at several points in the country. Brown coal, as the variety is known, has been found near the city of Ilobasco capital of the district of the same name, in the Department of Cabañas.

The railroads of Salvador comprise the Ferro Carril de Santa Ana, which is made up of the railway from the Port of Acajutla to Sonsorate, opened July 15, 1882. Its extension eastward from Sonsonate to Ateos, opened in 1886, was constructed by English capital, and the further extension, north from Ateos to Santa Ana, is now under contract, that reaching La Joya will be opened this August.

Moreover, a branch is proposed from Ateos eastwards to Santa Tecla, half of it already constructed by the Government, leaving only a few miles incomplete. This is under grading force directed by the Government employees.

A beautiful railway leading from Santa Tecla to San Salvador, has been completed and will be opened to traffic during the year. This is a private enterprise. The extension road from Ateos to Santa Ana belongs to the Government. There is a concession granted for a railroad from San Salvador to La Union, while the continuation of the same, from San Miguel to La Union is under way, and bids fair to be of great benefit to the public. It may be remarked that the parts of the Acajutla terminus of the Santa Ana Railway, as well as the adjoining port of La Libertad, are open road-steads, while La Union is a shelter harbor and a first-class port.

The data regarding the railroads of the Republic is obtained from valuable information given by Mr. A. J. Scherzer, a man of distinguished eminence in scientific pursuits and of most charming personality. He has done more for the Central American advancement than any foreign financier in the southern Republics, and deserves credit in every form for the work he has so consistently accomplished for the country and its people.

The extent of the Republic of Salvador, is placed at 7,255 square miles, and the population, as stated officially in 1891, at 777,895. The population, like that of most of the Republics of Central and South America, consists of the descendants of the Latin races, with some Indians and Negroes. There are of course some mixed races, known as Mestizos. The separate departments are controlled by a Governor and an alternate for each department with a General commandant, and the local affairs of each town are administered by an alcalde, a syndic and two or more magistrates, as may be determined by the number of the population, all these officers being elected directly by the people.

CHURCH AT PANCHIMALCO SALVADOR

San Salvador, "the city of our Saviour," the capital, was founded in 1528, and has now a population between twenty and thirty thousand. The other cities of importance are: Santa Ana, Sonsonate, San Vicente, Ahauchapan, San Miguel and Acoyapa. The Catholic religion prevails, but there is absolute religious freedom and toleration. In, the matter of education the progress is rapid. Besides a fine system of public schools largely attended, there are three universities and several flourishing colleges. Primary education is free and compulsory. There are fifteen or twenty periodicals published in the Republic, and they are very fair exponents of the enlightenment and advancement of the country. The capital contains a valuable and interesting museum and an extensive national library. The army is well disciplined and splendidly equipped, and is the best in Central America.

The resources of this teeming and beautiful country are numberless, new riches being discovered every year. It is absolutely so productive in its soil products, so affluent in its mineral treasures, that it might be unmoored from the outer world, for all time, and suffer no want or deprivation as to the actual needs of human life and most of its luxuries. The chief products are coffee, tobacco, sugar, indigo, cacao, woods and medicinal plants, though there are countless other crops, vegetable growths, shrubs and grains, with a long list of delicious fruits, fish and game birds. The mines are of gold, iron, silver, copper and mercury. The forests are rich and luxuriant, and flaming birds of splendid plumage brighten them like flocks of winged flowers.

The principal railway in operation at present is a line from Acajutla to Sonsonate, which is to extend to Amate Marin and thence to the capital. Those in course of construction or projected are to connect Acajutla and Santa Ana, La Union and San Miguel, La Libertad and San Salvador and La Union with the frontier towns of Guatemala. A tramway extends from San Salvador to Santa Tecla. The postal service is complete and efficient, the telegraphic communications extensive, and there are several hundred miles of telephone wires. The peso of one hundred centavos, equal to 64.9 cents, United States coin (July 1, 1892), is the monetary unit. The coins of England, Spain, France, United States and particularly the Peruvian soles and the

WHITE HOUSE

Chilian pesos circulate freely. One of the loveliest scenes on nature's vast canvas is a coffee plantation. The leaves of the plant are a very dark green, the flowers white and freighted with a rich aromatic incense, and the berries are red. These plantations in Salvador are numerous and wide in extent. They are cultivated with the utmost care and nicety—not a weed or blade of grass to be seen anywhere. The plants are set out in regular order and are of uniform size and height, so that they present an almost hedge-like appearance. In the natural state the plant attains a height of fifteen feet or more, but when cultivated is cut back to about six or seven. The shrub is drooping and graceful, the flowers as sweet as the jessamine. When the fruit is ripe it looks not unlike the cranberry in size and color. This fruit contains each only two seeds or berries, which are found close together, the flat sides touching, separated only by the thinnest tissue. The plant requires a good soil and plenty of shade; so necessary is the latter condition that shade trees, which branch out at the top, are often planted between the rows. Sometimes banana trees serve this purpose, and thus a double harvest is made. When the berries are gathered they are carried to a factory, where they are run through a pulping machine, which denudes the berry and carries off the refuse or pulp, which makes an excellent fertilizer. When the beans are washed and dried in the sun, they are then fanned or winnowed to free them of chaff or tissue, and they are then laboriously hand-picked and assorted into several grades. The labor in the fields is done by the men, that of the mills and sorting rooms by women and girls. Labor is cheap and plentiful, as in this abundant land food and clothing come without the stress and cruel burdens of countries that pride themselves on a more advanced civilization.

After coffee the most important agricultural products are cacao, sugar, maize and indigo. Cotton has been raised with ease and a fine yield, and will undoubtedly in time become a large source of revenue. Indigo is largely grown, and it requires a very large quantity of the plants to produce a pound of it. It is native to the soil ("Indigofera Disperma"). It flourishes almost everywhere, and its cultivation is very easy and simple—a clearing of the

PARK OF AHUACHAPAN, SALVADOR

CAMPO DEL MORTE

SOLDIERS OF SALVADOR

AND VIEW OF SANTA ANA.

SENIOR DON EDUARDO POIRIER,
Minister from Salvador to Mexico.

ground, shallow ploughing and the sowing of the seed broadcast being all that is necessary. This is done in the spring, and it grows and matures so quickly that by midsummer it is six feet high and ready for cutting. The first year the crop is not large, but the second year it is at the fullest yield. The first year's crop is called *tinta nueva*, the second *tinta retono*. As soon as it is cut the manufacture begins, and by November it is ready for market.

On the 28th of August last a very important enterprise was inaugurated with appropriate ceremonies. It was the opening of the "Central American Mint, Limited." The industry has been pushed with astonishing rapidity, and has made a most favorable impression of the pluck and energy of the British on the minds of the progressive Salvadorians. This country is making rapid strides in all the arts of peace, and President Ezeta's *régime* will long be remembered as an era of unusual advancement. When the National Mint is fully established a gold standard will be fixed in the country. The development of the mineral wealth is as yet in its infancy, and the eyes of the far-seeing capitalists of many nations are turned toward this little republic. They will find here not only nature's eldorado, but an intelligent people and a liberal government that will heartily co-operate in every effort that tends to the development of this glorious country.

And now to bid farewell to Salvador, not without regret, for I love the way the sun shines among the palm trees, the way the shadows extend along the high hills and mountains, the quiet lull of the noon-day heat, the cooling breezes that waft over the gloom of the evening, and I love the debonnair land of roses and love.

Salvador, home of heroes born, where they cast themselves with their swords into the heat of battle, to conquer or die—full of love for the land whose blood has imprinted on the forehead of many a soldier *Excelsior.*